REALLY HORRIBLE FACTS

REALLY HORRIBLE SCIENCE FACTS

Jay Hawkins

WINDMILL BOOKS

NEW YORK

Published in 2014 by Windmill Books, LLC
303 Park Avenue South, Suite # 1280, New York, NY 10010-3657

First Edition

Editors: Samantha Noonan, Deborah Kespert, Nicola Barber, and Joe Harris
US Editor: Joshua Shadowens
Illustrations: Dynamo Ltd, Quadrum, and Steve Beaumont
Layout design: Trudi Webb

Library of Congress Cataloging-in-Publication Data

Hawkins, Jay.
 Really horrible science facts / by Jay Hawkins.
    pages cm. -- (Really horrible facts)
 Includes index.
 ISBN 978-1-61533-745-3 (library binding) -- ISBN 978-1-61533-807-8 (pbk.) -- ISBN 978-1-61533-808-5 (6-pack)
1. Science--Miscellanea. I. Title.
 Q173.H39 2014
 500--dc23
                                       2012049812

Printed in China
CPSIA Compliance Information: Batch #AS3102WM:
For Further Information contact Windmill Books, New York, New York at 1-866-478-0556
SL002699US

CONTENTS

FOUL FOOD SCIENCE

Your body cannot digest tomato seeds—they pass straight through your intestines. Eat some today and see for yourself!

Although your gut contains powerful acids, they cannot digest chewing gum. Small amounts will get through the digestive system, but too much can cause a serious blockage... so always spit it out.

Some ancient Japanese monks wanted to become mummies. They ate a special diet to preserve their bodies after death: tree bark and roots, and poisonous tea.

Most of the food you eat spends between one and three hours in your stomach, but fatty foods hang around for longer.

If you eat a lot of beets, your urine can turn pink!

Many cheap meat products such as sausages and burgers are made from "mechanically separated meat." This is a meaty slime collected from washing bones and grinding up parts of the dead animal that aren't used for anything else.

In an emergency, coconut milk can be used as a substitute for the watery part of blood in a blood transfusion.

SICK SCIENCE

You're more likely to get sick from kissing another person than a dog. Even though a dog's mouth has as many germs as a human's, not as many of them are harmful to us.

The Japanese beetle, now common in the United States, can eat through a human eardrum.

Astronauts grow taller while they are in space. Their spines get longer, because they are no longer squashed up by gravity.

Scientists have recreated the deadly flu virus that killed one percent of the entire world population between 1918 and 1919. We hope it doesn't escape!

6

More than a billion people have a hookworm infection. That means they have tiny bloodsucking worms living in their intestines. All those hookworms suck a total of 22 million pints (10 million l) of blood per day!

Shaving a pregnant mouse makes her produce more milk and grow larger babies. A bald mouse can digest more food without overheating, and so makes more milk.

The first time that anyone saw a frog throwing up was when one was taken on a space flight.

7

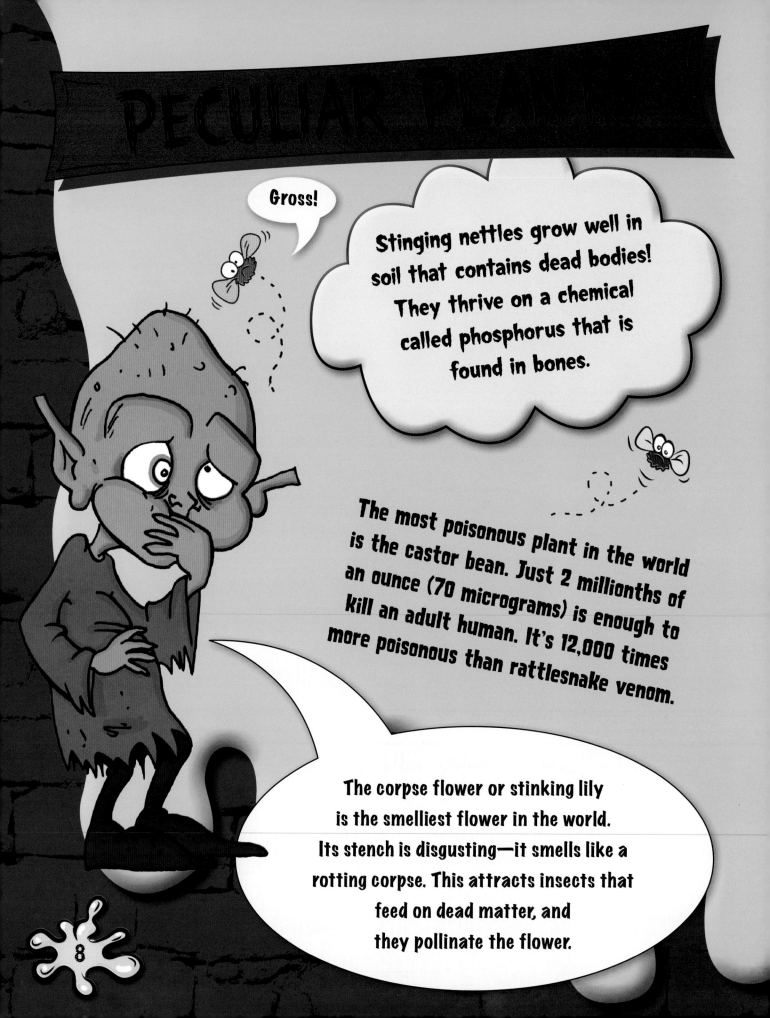

PECULIAR PLANTS

Gross!

Stinging nettles grow well in soil that contains dead bodies! They thrive on a chemical called phosphorus that is found in bones.

The most poisonous plant in the world is the castor bean. Just 2 millionths of an ounce (70 micrograms) is enough to kill an adult human. It's 12,000 times more poisonous than rattlesnake venom.

The corpse flower or stinking lily is the smelliest flower in the world. Its stench is disgusting—it smells like a rotting corpse. This attracts insects that feed on dead matter, and they pollinate the flower.

Yuck!

Some types of pitcher plants can "eat" birds and even rats. Animals are attracted by the nectar of the flower, and then fall into a vat of chemicals. The chemicals dissolve them, feeding the plant.

The Australian bloodwood tree oozes red sap that looks like blood when it is cut.

Some trees communicate using chemicals. If a wood-eating bug attacks one, the tree releases chemicals into the air, which prompt other trees in the area to produce a poison that deters the bugs.

ALIVE AND SQUIRMING

The largest living thing on Earth is a giant fungus that covers 4 square miles (10.4 sq km) in Oregon. It is thought to be around 2,400 years old, but may be as old as 8,650 years!

The anacampseros plant looks like bird poop. Its weird appearance protects it from being eaten by animals.

A mushroom from Africa, called the Lady in the Veil, grows faster than any other organism in the world. It grows up to 8 inches (20 cm) in only 20 minutes, and can be heard cracking as it grows!

In just ten years, a poisonous spider called the false widow has colonized southern England. It arrived in bunches of bananas, and warm weather has allowed it to survive. There are now tens of thousands of false widows running wild!

Parts of the Atacama Desert in Chile have had no rain for 400 years.

Some types of plants and animals have evolved to live inside volcanic vents, at the bottom of vast caves, and even deep under the sea.

Some fossilized cockroaches are 300 million years old. This means they existed 100 million years before the dinosaurs!

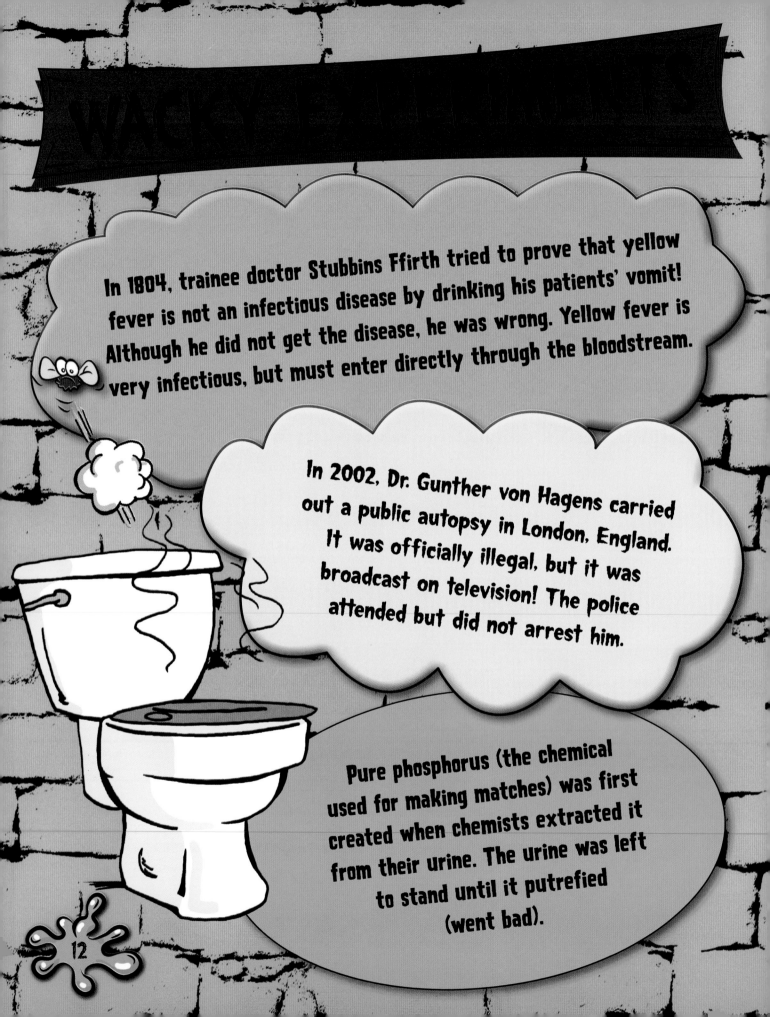

WACKY EXPERIMENTS

In 1804, trainee doctor Stubbins Ffirth tried to prove that yellow fever is not an infectious disease by drinking his patients' vomit! Although he did not get the disease, he was wrong. Yellow fever is very infectious, but must enter directly through the bloodstream.

In 2002, Dr. Gunther von Hagens carried out a public autopsy in London, England. It was officially illegal, but it was broadcast on television! The police attended but did not arrest him.

Pure phosphorus (the chemical used for making matches) was first created when chemists extracted it from their urine. The urine was left to stand until it putrefied (went bad).

NATURAL DISASTERS

The lava (molten rock) that erupts out of a volcano can be as hot as 2,200 degrees Fahrenheit (1,200 degrees C). The power of a large eruption can equal that of a million nuclear bombs.

Gross!

The Richter scale measures the size of an earthquake and normally goes from 1 (small) to 10 (massive). The largest earthquake ever recorded was a 9.5 in Chile, in 1960. An earthquake measuring 12 would break the Earth in half!

If you are trapped in an avalanche, you have a 93 percent chance of survival if you are rescued within 15 minutes. Some people have survived for longer than two hours.

A tsunami is a massive wave that sweeps over the land and destroys everything in its path. It can be 100 ft (30 m) high when it strikes the shore.

Yuck!

The Yellow River flood in China in 1931 is the deadliest known natural disaster. It killed between one million and four million people.

One of the largest volcanic eruptions recorded in recent history occurred on the island of Krakatau in Indonesia in 1883. It was so huge that most of the island disappeared into the sea!

WILD WEATHER

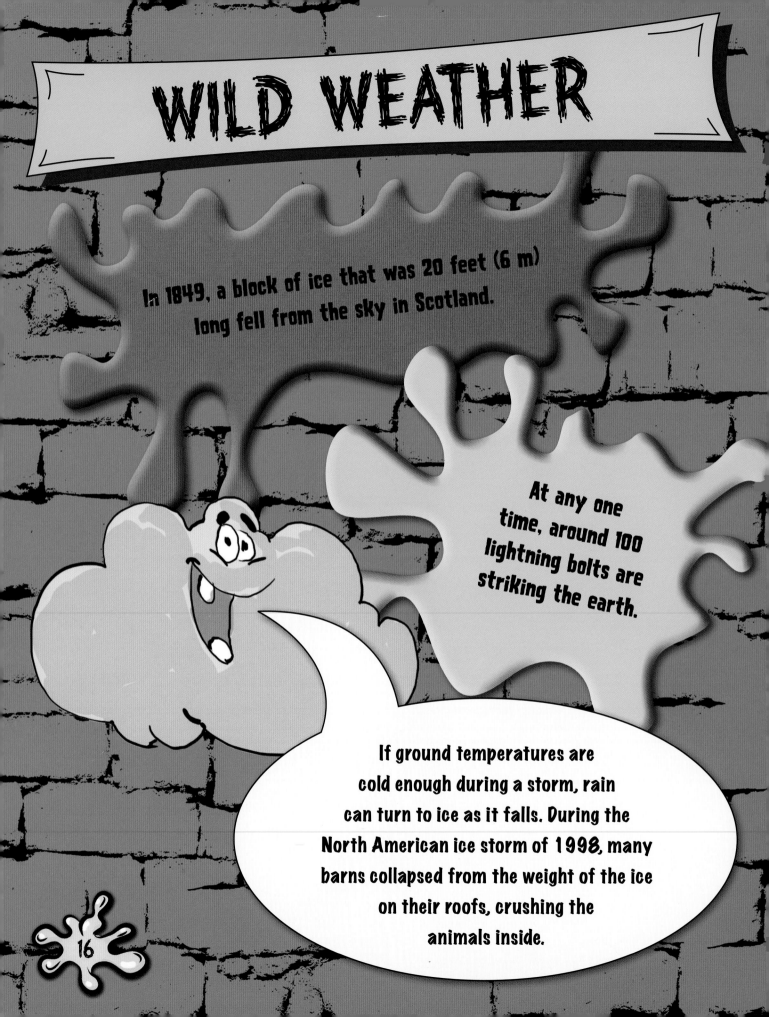

In 1849, a block of ice that was 20 feet (6 m) long fell from the sky in Scotland.

At any one time, around 100 lightning bolts are striking the earth.

If ground temperatures are cold enough during a storm, rain can turn to ice as it falls. During the North American ice storm of 1998, many barns collapsed from the weight of the ice on their roofs, crushing the animals inside.

A lightning bolt is five times hotter than the surface of the sun.

Acid rain is caused by industrial gases like sulfur dioxide. In highly industrialized areas, the pH level of acid rain can be lower than 2.4—more acidic than vinegar!

The frequency of major hurricanes and storms has doubled over the last hundred years, possibly as a result of climate change.

There have been rainstorms with falling fish, frogs, and toads!

MEDICAL MARVELS

Tom Thompson of Decatur, Georgia, holds the world record for having the largest metal plate ever inserted into a human skull. Made of titanium, the plate measures 15.9 by 4.3 inches (40 by 11 cm).

In the Middle Ages, doctors used leeches to remove "bad blood." Today, doctors still use leeches in some surgical procedures, as they produce chemicals that stop pain and keep blood flowing without clotting.

Early anatomists were not allowed to study dead bodies, so they paid grave robbers to steal them. Often, the bodies of executed criminals were stolen and sold.

In ancient times, Indian doctors used live ants to "stitch" wounds together. The doctor would hold the edges together and get the ant to bite through the skin. The ant's head would then be snapped off, leaving its jaws as the "stitch!"

Stone Age people used to practice "trepanning"—a medical procedure that involved drilling a hole in the skull. They had no anesthetics, so it must have hurt!

In the condition myiasis, maggots hatch out and live under the skin—they can even be seen wriggling around. In 1993, doctors in Boston developed a treatment for myiasis that involved covering the skin with bacon. Maggots like the bacon, so come up toward it. Doctors then pull them out with tweezers. Gross!

POTTY POISONS

Aconite is one of the most deadly poisons known—yet it is used in some homeopathic remedies as a "medicine!"

Gross!

Arsenic was so commonly used as a poison by murderers in the 1800s that a law was passed in Britain in 1840 that arsenic must be mixed with a blue or black dye so that people could see it in their food.

It takes less than 0.004 ounces (0.1 grams) of poison found in parts of the pufferfish to kill an adult human. However, in Japan, pufferfish is eaten as a delicacy!

Cyanide is a poison that can be made from several plants. A tiny amount is deadly in just five minutes.

Antifreeze is deadly poisonous. Some governments insist that manufacturers add a chemical to make it taste horrible to stop people and animals from drinking it.

Yuck!

Strychnine poisoning causes extreme muscle spasms. They can be so severe that the body can jerk backward until the heels touch the back of the head and the face is drawn into a terrifying, wide, fixed grin.

The taste of rat poison varies in different countries. It is adapted to suit the food rats are most used to.

LOOKING PRETTY

Some people want their tongues to be forked, like snake tongues. A scalpel or laser is used to cut down the middle of the tongue and give it a forked appearance. Freaky!

Some toiletries and makeup products contain carmine, a coloring made from crushed beetles!

Erl Van Aken is really into body modification. He has a flap of skin on his stomach formed into a kind of handle shape that he can put his finger through.

Some women belonging to the Kayan people of Burma wear rings around their necks from the age of two. More and more rings are added as they get older. This changes the way their bones grow, and makes their necks appear stretched!

Australian performance artist Stelarc had a human ear grafted onto his forearm in the name of art. He can literally turn a deaf ear to anyone who annoys him!

Some cultures have a tradition of earlobe stretching: people wear heavy earrings that can weigh up to a pound (0.45 kg). The weight of the earrings pulls the earlobes down, leaving huge holes.

Japanese scientists have discovered a way of extracting a vanilla-like fragrance from manure that could be used in cosmetics. Get ready for cow-dung bubble bath!

TECHNOLOGY GOES NUTS

Earthrace is said to be the world's fastest eco-boat. It's partly powered by human fat from its crew members!

A dentist from New York invented the electric chair.

A robotic caterpillar can be used in heart surgery. It is inserted through a small hole in the chest, and crawls over a person's heart to inject drugs.

There are over 20,000 car crashes involving kangaroos in Australia every year, so a robotic kangaroo-like crash test dummy, called Robo-Roo, is used to test how badly cars will be damaged.

Chemical engineers have developed a spray-on skin for soldiers. The special goo is designed to cover troops' wounds in war zones and can last for up to two weeks.

Amazonian hunters heat poison arrow frogs over a fire to sweat the poison out of them. They use the poison to tip their hunting arrows.

Robotarium X, in Portugal, is the world's first robot zoo. The 45 robots share a steel and glass cage. Some are nice, and respond to visitors. Others are nasty and bite the tails off their companions. How bizarre!

SHOCKING SPACE

Astronauts wear diapers during takeoff, landing, and on space walks because they can't go to the bathroom at these times!

Gross!

The effects of zero gravity on the human body are so severe that astronauts who stay in space for a long time suffer muscle wasting and loss of bone density. They can be unwell for months or sometimes years after their return to Earth.

If you fell into a black hole, your body would be "spaghettified"— drawn out into an incredibly long, thin strand. Better not try!

The National Aeronautics and Space Administration (NASA), founded in 1958, has developed ways to collect sweat from exercising astronauts to convert into drinking water for them in space. They can also do this with urine!

The "Vomit Comet" is the name given to an aircraft that flies in a way that makes people weightless. It's used to train astronauts, carry out research, and even make movies. It tends to make people sick, as you could probably guess...

Solid waste from bathrooms on space shuttles is squashed down and stored for return to Earth. Liquid waste is thrown out into space.

Yuck!

CRAZY SCIENTISTS

A "body farm" is a research center where dead bodies are left to decay in various situations. Scientists study them and the information is used to help police with murder investigations.

Scientists are experimenting with a pill made from the same material as disposable diapers to help people lose weight, The pill expands to 1,000 times its original size, making the person feel full, so they don't eat.

British scientists have found that a robotic nose is better at detecting smells if it is given a coating of fake snot!

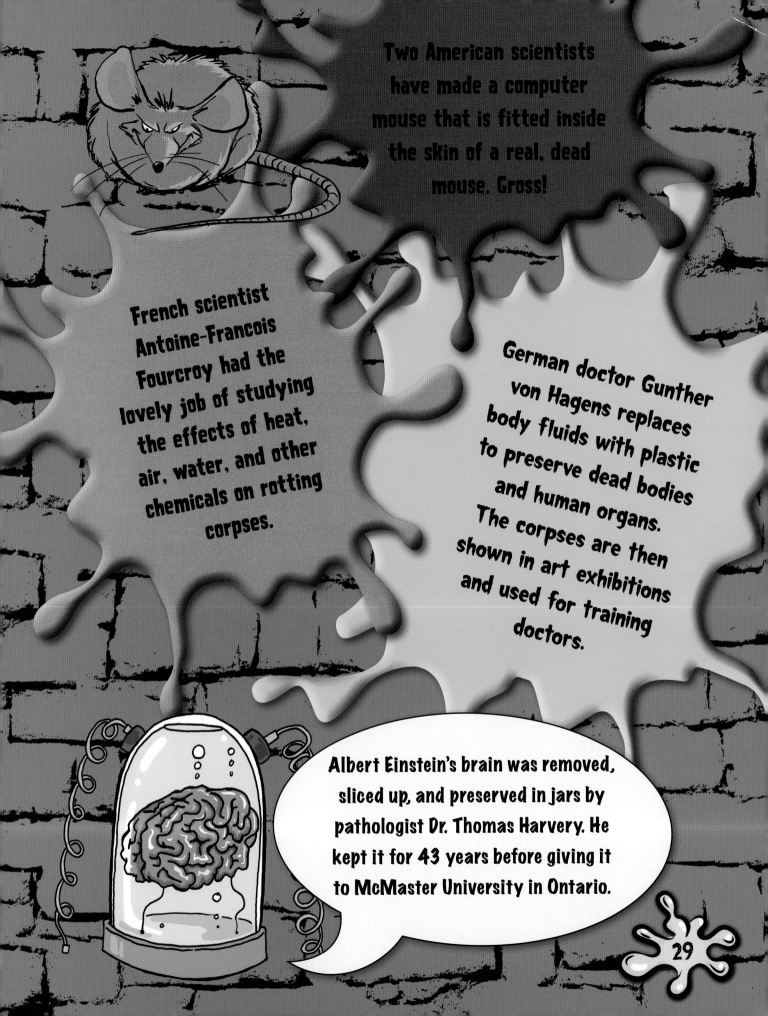

Two American scientists have made a computer mouse that is fitted inside the skin of a real, dead mouse. Gross!

French scientist Antoine-Francois Fourcroy had the lovely job of studying the effects of heat, air, water, and other chemicals on rotting corpses.

German doctor Gunther von Hagens replaces body fluids with plastic to preserve dead bodies and human organs. The corpses are then shown in art exhibitions and used for training doctors.

Albert Einstein's brain was removed, sliced up, and preserved in jars by pathologist Dr. Thomas Harvery. He kept it for **43** years before giving it to McMaster University in Ontario.

INVENTIONS AND DISCOVERIES

In 2006, a slime-based device was invented for controlling crowds. It shoots a stream of slime at troublemakers so that they slip and fall over, finding it impossible to get up again!

Joseph Gayetty produced the first factory-made toilet paper in New York in 1857—he was so pleased with his product that he had his name printed on every sheet!

In 1863, American inventor William Bullock helped to revolutionize the printing industry with his web rotary printing press. In a bizarre accident, Bullock was killed by his own invention when he became caught up in one of his machines.

It's an urban myth that Thomas Crapper invented the flushing toilet! He was simply a successful 19th-century London plumber with his own brand of toilets.

30

Fritz von Opel, a German car builder, became the first person to fly by rocket power in 1929. He stayed in the air for 75 seconds!

The yo-yo was invented in the Philippines centuries ago—possibly for use as a weapon! Its history as a children's toy began in 1928 when Pedro Flores opened a yo-yo factory in California.

Eight-year-old Christopher James Wolfe discovered Zuniceratops in 1996 in New Mexico. You're never too young to start dinosaur hunting!

GLOSSARY

anatomist (uh-NA-tuh-mist) Someone who studies the structure of living things.

anesthetics (a-nus-THET-iks) Drugs that stop you feeling pain temporarily.

autopsy (AW-top-see) Cutting up a corpse to find out how the person died.

gastric (GAS-trik) Of the stomach.

intestines (in-TES-tinz) The tubes in your belly that digest your food.

pH level (PEE AYTCH LEH-vul) A measure of acidity.

transfusion (tranz-FYOO-zhun) Replacing blood.

FURTHER READING

Korman, Susan. *Sid the Science Kid: Why Did My Ice Pop Melt?* New York: HarperFestival, 2010.

Murphy, Glenn. *How Loud Can You Burp?* New York: Roaring Brook Press, 2009.

Wells, Robert E. *Why Do Elephants Need the Sun?* Park Ridge, IL: Albert Whitman & Co., 2012.

WEBSITES

For web resources related to the subject of this book, go to: www.windmillbooks.com/weblinks and select this book's title.

INDEX